Original title:
Shadows of Sass and Snickers

Copyright © 2025 Creative Arts Management OÜ
All rights reserved.

Author: Evan Hawthorne
ISBN HARDBACK: 978-1-80567-451-1
ISBN PAPERBACK: 978-1-80567-750-5

The Cheeky Twilight Chronicles

In the glow of the streetlamp's gleam,
A raccoon steals snacks from a dream.
With a wink and a sly little grin,
He tiptoes away, letting the night begin.

The moon chuckles at his bold little act,
As crickets join in with a playful tact.
Who knew mischief could glow so bright,
In this realm of giggles that dance through the night?

Revelry Beyond the Dusk

When the sun dips low, the antics begin,
With owls hooting tunes to the night's whim.
The fireflies flicker, like jester's delight,
While the stars roll their eyes at the comedic sight.

A cat chases shadows, all fluff and no grace,
Tripping and tumbling, what a funny chase!
Laughter bursts forth from the dark, sparkling sea,
As giggles echo where none can see.

Riddles Wrapped in Gloom

In a park where the whispers play hide and seek,
A ghost with a care for mischief, unique.
He offers up riddles, seasoned with jest,
Leaving wanderers puzzled, a curious quest.

The bats start to giggle, their wings light with fun,
While shadows create stories, one by one.
In the heart of the dark, there's a chuckle or two,
As the night unfolds with a surreal view.

Playful Shadows Dancing

Underneath the porch light, the shadows do sway,
Frolicking about in a whimsical play.
A squirrel in a top hat gives a bow to the crowd,
As laughter erupts, drawing all who are proud.

A jolly old dog prances, with flair in his step,
Chasing his tail, oh, what a misstep!
Moonbeams twinkle as they partner with glee,
In this celestial ball where all are carefree.

Frivolous Footprints

Little footprints dance in the sand,
Giggling whispers from a curious band.
Waves of laughter crash and roll,
Each step a tickle, a funny stroll.

Sandy shoes and silly faces,
Chasing shadows, they win all the races.
Jumps and splashes, light on their toes,
Footprints left where hilarity flows.

Fleeting moments under the sun,
Exchanging jokes, oh what fun!
Puddles of laughter, rolling in glee,
With each crack, a new joke's decree.

The Charm of Offhand Remarks

A sharp-tongued friend with a wink in the eye,
Delivers a punchline while passing by.
Witty banter on a sunny day,
Leaves them giggling in the funniest way.

Casual jests that catch you off guard,
Words that twirl like a dancing bard.
Each quip a sprinkle, a dash of delight,
Serving up laughter in the soft twilight.

The Laughter Tucked Beneath Stars

Under the sky where the whimsy beams,
Silly stories unfold like dreams.
Crickets chirp in rhythm divine,
As chuckles bubble like a fine wine.

Moonlit giggles float in the air,
Cuddled joy beyond compare.
Hidden treasures in jokes well spun,
Laughter blooming like flowers, just begun.

Laughing in the Half-Light

Flickering shadows dance on the wall,
With every chuckle, the night starts to call.
Jesters' tales told with flair and fun,
In the half-light, laughter's never done.

Teasing glances, mischievous grins,
In this playful realm, everyone wins.
With jokes that pop like fireworks bright,
The magic of laughter illuminates the night.

Whispers of Witty Whimsy

In the corner, a jester does prance,
With a wig that's awry, he takes a chance.
His jokes take flight on a unicycle,
A giggle, a snort, it's quite the spectacle.

In a world full of frowns, he turns the tide,
With a wink, a pun, oh, what a ride!
His hat's too large, but his heart is bright,
Chasing away gloom with pure delight.

Gloaming Glares and Grins

When twilight falls, the quirky appear,
With tales so tall, they ignite cheer.
A dog in a top hat spins around,
While laughter erupts from the lost and found.

A tickle of breeze carries secrets to share,
Of spoons that dance, and socks with flair.
Each giggle rises like bubbles in air,
Painting the dusk with a jubilant glare.

Echoes of Eccentric Laughter

In a bustling cafe, the oddballs meet,
With pastries piled high, oh what a treat!
One claims his cake can sing a tune,
While another juggles grapes with a spoon.

They trade silly tales of hiccups and falls,
With snorts and cackles that echo off walls.
A toast to the quirky, the mad and the fun,
Where laughter's a race, and everyone's won.

Twilight Tease and Tickle

As dusk settles in, they gather near,
With glances that twinkle, sparking cheer.
A whisper of fun floats through the air,
With playful nudges and jokes to spare.

A squirrel in a suit struts by with flair,
Conducting a choir of birds unaware.
They chuckle aloud at a night so bizarre,
Where every moment is a twinkling star.

The Rhythms of Raucous Laughter

Beneath the bright and blinking stars,
The giggles dance like buzzing cars.
Laughter tumbles, flips and rolls,
Tickling hearts and warming souls.

In corners dark, a whisper plays,
A jest that shimmers, never strays.
With cheeky grins like daring sprights,
They bounce and bounce through joyful nights.

The jester's hat, a twinkling sight,
Winks mischief with every bite.
As puns and riddles fill the air,
We float in joy, without a care.

A raucous toast to silly dreams,
Where laughter bubbles, purples, creams.
In the night's embrace we sway,
To rhythms bold that lead the way.

Enigmatic Chuckles

A laugh that echoes in the breeze,
Hides secrets in the rustling trees.
With every turn, surprise unfolds,
In giggles wrapped, a tale retold.

Lurking jesters tease the moon,
As subtle tricks make muggles swoon.
Each chuckle dances, twirls in flight,
A whimsical laugh, a curious sight.

The playful whispers softly land,
In corners dim, they expand,
Crafting joy from shadows near,
A riddle-clear, yet fluffy cheer.

Cackles chase the twinkling stars,
While clever quips are brewed in jars.
The night wears smiles, a playful coat,
Where echoes spark with every note.

Twists of the Cheeky Moon

When the moon beams with a cheeky grin,
Its giggles tickle like a playful sin.
Stars play games in the cosmic dance,
Mirthful glances with a wink of chance.

Echoing laughter leaps from sight,
As shadows twirl in sheer delight.
The night unfolds its giddy schemes,
We chase the rhythm of our dreams.

With each misstep, a laughter-glow,
We spin in joy, all part of the show.
In this moonlit affair, we find
The threads of humor intertwined.

So come and play 'neath the moon's embrace,
Where funny tales weave and chase.
Amidst the giggles and cheeky sighs,
Our laughter echoes through the skies.

The Nocturnal Jest

When night unfurls its starry cloak,
A jest awakens, laughter spoke.
In twilight's grip, the giggles grow,
A merry band begins to flow.

They dash through alleys, quick and spry,
With leaps and bounds beneath the sky.
Each wink a riddle, each grin a tease,
As shadows sway like playful leaves.

A siren's laugh, a joker's call,
Inviting all to join the ball.
Together we swirl in a light-hearted jest,
In winks and chuckles, we find our rest.

So let's embrace the mirthful night,
Where punchlines bloom and glee takes flight.
For in this world of jesting glee,
We are all stars, unbound and free.

Sassy Sunsets

The sky wears a wink, all orange and pink,
As giggles escape from a slinky old sink.
Clouds float like jesters, in puffy parade,
While the sun gives a smirk, never afraid.

With colors that dance, the horizon's a tease,
The light plays tricks, it aims to please.
As night drapes a robe, full of dandy delight,
Even stars chuckle softly, igniting the night.

The Lightness of Snide Comments

Whispers like feathers, soft but so sharp,
Banter that twinkles like strings of a harp.
With each roll of the eyes, laughter takes flight,
A chorus of giggles as wrong feels so right.

Remarks that are cheeky, float through the air,
Like marshmallows tossed, with naught but a care.
In a world full of smirks, the humor ignites,
As snide little quips dance like firefly lights.

The Secret Life of Frivolous Whispers

In corners they gather, those whispers so spry,
With tales of mischief that flit and that fly.
Like butterflies giggling, they flurry about,
Crafting soft chaos, with giggles and clout.

They'll whisper a secret, then burst into song,
A symphony silly, where all things belong.
In the hush of the night, they play hide and seek,
With chortles that ripple, brightening bleak.

Smirks and Sneers Under the Moon

Beneath the moon's gaze, some sneaky and sly,
Join shadows that stretch, as they flit and they fly.
With gleeful intentions, they share a sly grin,
As stars find the courage to join in the din.

In laughter and twirls, mischief takes hold,
Each smirk holds a story, each sneer keeps it bold.
For in the night's mischief, the fun never ends,
As light-hearted giggles weave magic with friends.

Smirking Under the Streetlamp

In the glow where the mischief creeps,
Laughter dances, and the corner peeps.
A glint of humor in the pale light spark,
Witty whispers spill like a playful lark.

A cat struts by with a cheeky prance,
Tail flicks in rhythm, a sarcastic dance.
The lamplight chuckles, flickering bright,
As jokes tumble out, igniting the night.

The Twinkle in Mirth's Depths

Beneath the moon's playful gaze,
Giggling echoes twist through the haze.
Each chuckle that bounces on cool, crisp air,
Unleashes a joy, a comedic affair.

Stars wink in sync with the banter of friends,
As punchlines pirouette, laughter ascends.
Grins take flight, like balloons in the sky,
As we toast to the humor that makes spirits fly.

Toes Tapping in Twilight's Embrace

The sun dips low, painting the scene,
With giggles and jeers, a jovial sheen.
Toes tap to the rhythm of dusk's soft song,
While puns weave around, inviting the throng.

A breeze carries whispers, a teasing delight,
As we dance to the tune, hearts light as the night.
Where the shadows play tricks and humor will bloom,
In this whimsical world, joy must resume.

The Jestful Edge of Evening

When twilight descends with a playful smirk,
Every corner is giddy, as giggles lurk.
The air's thick with jests, zany and spry,
As wit takes the wheel, and we simply fly.

With whimsy afloat on the breeze that we share,
We snicker in harmony, shedding all care.
The dusk transforms, illuminating the fun,
In the jestful embrace, our hearts become one.

Murmurs of the Playful Night

Whispers dance among the trees,
Laughter floats upon the breeze.
A raccoon juggles with delight,
Moonbeams tickle through the night.

The owls chuckle, wise and slow,
While fireflies put on a show.
A cat in shades, so sly and neat,
Tips over cans, a grand repeat.

A stroll through jokes, a playful spree,
The night a canvas, wild and free.
Each corner hides a chuckle bright,
With every step, the giggles bite.

Under the stars, we share the glee,
In every shadow, a mystery.
With winks exchanged and grins so tight,
We cultivate this playful night.

The Drollness of Dusk

As daylight fades, the jesters rise,
With twinkling stars, mischief flies.
Frogs suit up in their best green,
Croaking tunes that can't be seen.

The wind, a bard with tales to tell,
Of socked feet that stumbled well.
A squirrel dons a tiny hat,
Surveying all with a knowing pat.

Beneath the moon, the pranks unfold,
With every giggle, new stories told.
A dance of shadows, quick and sly,
Leaves tickling as they pass by.

Embrace the dusk, with laughter's call,
In this sweet madness, we all fall.
Each chirp and rustle, such a tease,
The drollness wraps us like a breeze.

Joking in Half-Light

In the half-light, secrets play,
With every giggle on display.
A firefly sparks with a cheeky grin,
As crickets join in on the din.

The shadows weave their tangled pranks,
While moonlit giggles fill the banks.
A lost shoe takes a bow unfurled,
In this raucous, whimsical world.

Two mice chat about the cheese,
While drowsy bats hang with ease.
Each corner hides a sly retort,
As laughter echoes, our farcical sport.

Together we revel, no time to waste,
In this carnival of comic haste.
With every chuckle, a moment's delight,
Joking freely in the half-light.

The Quintessence of Snickered Wits

In corners dark, where giggles thrive,
The essence of wit comes alive.
With chuckles light and spirits that lift,
We sip on laughter, our favored gift.

Timing is key in this jesting game,
With every wink, it's never the same.
An acorn tumbles, a bonkers sight,
While raccoons plot their midnight bite.

The moon's a witness to our shenanigans,
As hedgehogs play with puns and plans.
We skedaddle through the twinkling grass,
Preserving humor as moments pass.

In this gathering of merry delight,
The quintessence swirls from day to night.
Join in the fun, where laughter fits,
In the grand parade of snickered wits.

The Sly Play of Words

In a world where whispers dance,
Puns prance like they've found romance.
A chuckle here, a giggle there,
Laughter threads through the playful air.

Jokes pirouette on tipsy toes,
While clever winks steal the show.
Hidden jests in every phrase,
Inventive minds set hearts ablaze.

Gloaming Giggles

As daylight fades in hues of glee,
Mirth spills out, wild and free.
Chortles echo through the night,
As jests take wing, oh what a sight!

Sticky puddles of pure delight,
Mischief dances with sheer might.
Lively banter fills the air,
In every glance, a playful flair.

The Radiance of Cheeky Remarks

Wit glimmers like stars above,
Spurring giggles, a playful shove.
Each quip is a spark of light,
Filling hearts with sheer delight.

Jests tumble down like autumn leaves,
Casting spells that no one believes.
Bright eyes shimmer with each tease,
Wit, the breeze that brings us ease.

Saucy Spirits at Dusk

Dusk brings whispers and shenanigans,
With playful nudges and clever plans.
Sardonic grins light up the night,
As laughter blooms, a sheer delight.

Banter rolls like a lively stream,
In the glow of mischief's dream.
Every jest a cheeky dance,
Where humor finds its perfect chance.

The Unsung Humorists

In corners where giggles stay,
The jesters dance, come out to play.
Their antics light the dullest days,
With quirky tales in funny ways.

They poke and prod with giddy grace,
A wink, a grin upon each face.
Their crafts are pure, an artful chase,
A snicker here, a laugh to trace.

When others sigh, they fan the flame,
With silly songs and jokes to claim.
They know that life's a playful game,
And laughter is their sweetest fame.

So let us cheer for those unseen,
The merry ones who keep life keen.
With laughter spilling from the scene,
They weave the fun in all between.

Jests in the Afterglow

When twilight falls and jesters rise,
The laughter echoes, fills the skies.
With every joke, the world complies,
A chorus of giggles, no goodbyes.

Late night banter, spirits bright,
They twist the tales, oh what a sight.
With witticisms that take flight,
And every punchline feels just right.

In the glow of moonlit cheer,
Each quip draws near, ignites the sphere.
They share a laugh, dispel the fear,
As chuckles linger, crystal clear.

So sip and savor, let it show,
Each jest is staged, a vibrant flow.
In laughter's warmth, our hearts aglow,
To humor's call, we all bestow.

Echoes of Jesting Shadows

Whispers float on midnight air,
Where laughter hides, it flourishes rare.
With playful jabs and witty flare,
The jesters thrive, without a care.

In darkened rooms, the fun unfolds,
Each snicker shared, a story told.
With every nod, the humor molds,
And life's absurdities grow bold.

Timid hearts transformed to brave,
As jests twist tales upon the wave.
A moment caught, we dance and save,
The joy we find, our spirits pave.

So heed the call of laughter's song,
In echoes bright where we belong.
With every pun, we'll laugh along,
In joyful harmony, we are strong.

The Art of Cheek

With raised brows and playful quirks,
They push the bounds with merry smirks.
Each cheeky jest, a spark that perks,
The dullest minds, it surely works.

In every corner, giggles bloom,
With wit as bright as flowers loom.
They turn the mundane into zoom,
Creating joy that sweeps the room.

A wink, a nudge, a prompt to play,
With every quip, they lead the way.
In laughter's light, we'll dance and sway,
A cheeky bond that won't decay.

So raise a toast to this fine art,
The laughter flows, it's pure and smart.
In every joke, we find our part,
A cheeky grin, a joyous heart.

Jests in the Half-Light

In the twilight, giggles grow,
Laughter dances, stealing the show.
Whispers tease the timid trees,
Jokes bounce like a warm summer breeze.

A cat in a hat sings out a tune,
Making old grumps start to swoon.
With every chuckle, the night gets bright,
Tricky words flutter, a playful flight.

Chortlings echo from door to door,
Humor spills out, we all want more.
Here, the frowns fade into quaint sighs,
As laughter weaves into starry skies.

So gather round in the dimming light,
Share a quip and take flight tonight.
For in this glow where fun begins,
A jest in the half-light always wins!

Revels of Resilient Rhetoric

In the realm of wit, we find our glee,
With clever quips as bright as can be.
Words juggle wildly, a playful spree,
Crafting laughter, just you and me.

Banter flies like birds on high,
With playful pokes that never die.
A pun lands softly, a giggle's spark,
Turning the mundane into a lark.

Bold jesters roam with mischievous glee,
Planting smiles where none used to be.
In this arena, we're all so wise,
Subtle jibes and bright, playful lies.

So raise your voice, let the fun ignite,
In the revels of words, we find our light.
With resilient rhetoric, we take a stand,
Sharing laughter, hand in hand.

Chortles Beneath the Moon

Under the moon's silvery glare,
Laughter spills like secrets in the air.
A frog in a suit cracks a joke so neat,
While stars above join in the beat.

Cackles rise like balloons at play,
Each chuckle a dancer swept away.
The night is young, and so are we,
With giggles echoing from tree to tree.

Silly stories swirl in delight,
As shadows prance in the soft moonlight.
With every punchline, spirits soar,
In this whimsical world, who could ask for more?

So let your heart be light and free,
Join the chortles, just you and me.
Beneath the moon, let laughter invade,
Creating memories that will never fade.

The Subtle Shade of Jest

In corners where the whispers dwell,
A subtle jest spins its own spell.
With twinkling eyes, we weave and play,
Crafting smiles in a cheeky way.

A wink, a nudge, the cleverest tease,
Setting the stage with effortless ease.
In this shade, let chuckles flow,
Wit like water, refreshing and slow.

Table talk becomes a grand affair,
With giggles shared in the soft night air.
Here, a slipped word causes a stir,
While hearts grow warm, it's quite a blur.

So gather close as the fun unfolds,
In the subtle shade, where laughter molds.
Each jest a treasure, bright and rare,
In this playful dance, there's joy to spare.

Innuendos and Illusions

Whispers dance on a breeze,
Quick glances spark the tease.
Jokes wrapped in a subtle sly,
Mirth blooms, oh my, oh my!

Laughter lingers in the air,
Giggling hearts without a care.
One-liners fly like shooting stars,
In this world, all laughter's ours!

Clever quips bring delight,
Innuendo sets the night.
Eyes twinkle with a playful glance,
In the game of jest, we prance!

So come, take part, join the fun,
With every pun, we're never done.
Life's comedic joy, we embrace,
Happiness woven in every space!

The Enchantment of Witty Banter

A wink exchanged in a crowded room,
Sparks fly, dispelling gloom.
With a quip, the tension breaks,
In this banter, laughter wakes.

Words that twist and turn with glee,
Innuendo, oh, so free!
Every jest, a playful art,
Creating smiles, a work of heart.

In the corridors of jest, we roam,
Finding joy far from the norm.
Jesting jests, oh what a treat,
Lively chatter, our hearts compete.

So let the laughter fill the air,
For wit and charm beyond compare.
In this magical verbal dance,
We twirl away in a comic trance!

Ripples of Merriment

Tickling fancies with every phrase,
Found in laughter's sunlit haze.
A jest ricochet, a smile unfolds,
Banter bright, worth more than gold.

From quips that sparkle like fine wine,
To playful nudges, all align.
Every chuckle swells the tide,
In waves of joy, we take our ride.

With a wink and a nudging grin,
Merriment's where we begin.
Echoes of laughter bounce around,
In this silliness, joy is found.

So gather 'round and let it flow,
As ripples spread, our spirits glow.
Each giggle we share brightly lights,
Our playful hearts on this funny night!

Glittering Gags

A prankster's smile, oh how it gleams,
Crafting humor beyond our dreams.
With every twist, the laughter grows,
In every jest, the magic flows.

Jokes, like jewels, catch the light,
Shining brightly, pure delight.
A playful jab, a clever pun,
In this arena, we all have fun!

So gather 'round for the comic show,
Where giggles twinkle, joy can grow.
Each gag delivered with flair and zing,
In this carnival of jest, we sing!

The laughter sparkles, the mood is bright,
In every punchline, sheer delight.
So let us celebrate the art of wit,
In this glittering world, we all commit!

The Language of Laughter

In corners of jest, giggles do thrive,
A symphony of chuckles, alive and sly.
Each wink a signal, each snort a glide,
In the dance of the mirthful, we take our ride.

With quips and jibes, we spin the tale,
A parade of smiles, where wrinkles prevail.
The secrets of joy, in whispers exchanged,
In the saga of laughter, we feel unchained.

A poke and a jab, the antics abound,
With playful mischief, in antics we're crowned.
We share a banquet of jokes, flavors bright,
Where the feast is of giggles and laughter's delight.

In this merry circus, we forge our crew,
With raucous applause, our friendship rings true.
In the theater of glee, we revel and play,
Creating a world where jest leads the way.

Cunning in the Glow

With glints in our eyes, plans start to brew,
Crafting schemes that tickle, all mockery true.
Each laugh is a puzzle, each grin a quest,
Playing tricks in the light, we jest at our best.

In whispers so sly, we plot our next jest,
Where humor's a treasure, buried in jest.
Like shadows that wink, we dance in our glee,
Cunning and quick, as wild as can be.

A burst of delight as our antics collide,
With chuckles and giggles, we sweep along wide.
In this raucous brigade, our spirits ignite,
Cunning in glow, we conquer the night.

Bound by our laughter, a playful brigade,
The bond of our banter, a charade well-played.
In rumbles of joy, we proudly exclaim,
Together we shine, in laughter's great name.

The Essence of Shimmering Humor

In the glimmer of jest, we float like a dream,
Sipping on chuckles, life's bubbling cream.
With a pinch of mirth, and a dash of delight,
Our spirits take wing, in the laughter-filled night.

A wink and a nudge, we craft tales so grand,
With humor's soft touch, we gather the band.
In whimsical worlds, where giggles unfold,
We dance in the light, with stories retold.

Laughter is nectar, a sweetened refrain,
In gardens of folly, we blossom again.
With whispers of joy, sprinkled like dew,
We bask in the truth that humor is true.

So here's to the mirth, in every small scheme,
To the essence of laughter, a radiant beam.
For in our adventures, both silly and bright,
We find in the chuckles, our shared delight.

Glimmering Guffaws

In the twilight's embrace, where jests take their flight,
Glimmers of laughter burst forth in the night.
Each guffaw a spark, ignites in the gloom,
We twirl through the echoes, where humor finds room.

With banter and wit, we orchestrate cheer,
In the symphony of snickers, we gather near.
Our voices blend melodies of whimsy and fun,
Under the moonlight, our laughter outruns.

With playful capers, our stories unfold,
Each twist and turn, a jest bold and bold.
In delightful mischief, we savor the game,
Glimmering guffaws igniting our flame.

So gather around, in this merry charade,
Where humor's the king, and laughter won't fade.
In the realm of the funny, we soar up so high,
In the glimmer of guffaws, together we fly.

Covert Chuckles in the Dark

In corners where the giggles creep,
The silent jesters watch and peep.
With playful grins behind the door,
They whisper secrets, evermore.

A boy in socks glides down the hall,
Each step a chance to trip and fall.
The laughter bubbles up like brew,
In darkened space, a playful crew.

A shadow dances on the wall,
It mimics moves, a silly sprawl.
With winks and nudges, they conspire,
To set the room ablaze with fire.

So let the night be filled with cheer,
As laughter looms, we persevere.
In friendly jests and playful blights,
The covert chuckles take their flights.

The Iridescent Gloom of Wit

In twilight's grip, the laughter stings,
As humor sprouts on vibrant wings.
An owl with glasses reads the room,
In iridescent hues it blooms.

The tickled cat with twitching tail,
Prowls through jokes like a nightingale.
Each chuckle echoes, bounces back,
From twilight's shade, a jolly track.

A ghost in slippers, soft and light,
Sneaks past the rest with pure delight.
With sighs and smiles, they take a chance,
To jig and jive in twilight dance.

The gloom's a canvas for our hearts,
In every crevice, jest imparts.
With wit that's sharp yet warm and bright,
We paint the night with glee and light.

Veils of Humor and Hilarity

Behind the curtain, laughter lies,
With veils of humor, glowing eyes.
Each tease concealed, a playful trick,
Beneath the surface, quips are thick.

A jester hops like bouncy bread,
With floppy shoes on silly tread.
The mirth entwined in every glance,
A tapestry of pure romance.

A pop of laughter fills the space,
As thoughts collide in funny race.
With giggles tucked in whispered trails,
Through these veils, the laughter sails.

So join the dance of pure delight,
In veils that shimmer, day and night.
For humor weaves a cherished bond,
In threads of joy, our hearts respond.

Glimmers in the Gloomy Hour

When night descends and worries creep,
The glimmers spark, awake from sleep.
A ticklish breeze whispers along,
The gloomiest hour hums a song.

The moonlight glints on playful pranks,
As laughter flows in silken flanks.
With jokes that twirl like curling mist,
They dance and mingle, none can resist.

In every shadow, tales abound,
A whispered jest, a joyful sound.
The clock strikes twelve, the fun ignites,
A parade of laughter claims the nights.

So fear not gloom, let giggles soar,
For in the dark, there's so much more.
With every glimmer brightly cast,
The funny moments hold us fast.

Jokes Drifting in Twilight

In the twilight, giggles roam,
Whispers of folly find a home.
Under the glow of the setting sun,
Laughter echoes, oh what fun!

Cheeky grins and playful jests,
Tickle the air, inviting guests.
Nibbling on snacks, they share a joke,
In this twilight, silliness awoke.

As twilight drips into night's embrace,
Every chuckle finds its place.
With a wink and a mischievous cheer,
The humor flows, loud and clear.

So gather round, and take your stand,
In this silly, lively band.
For as the day meets night's delight,
Jokes drift softly, making it right.

Mischief Beneath the Surface

Beneath the calm, a smirk will rise,
Brewing mischief in disguise.
Winks exchanged, a secret pact,
Laughter ready, that's a fact.

Who's the prankster? Who's the fool?
Giggles bubbling in the pool.
As the moon casts its playful gaze,
The night ignites in joyful craze.

Underneath the stars, we plot,
With every whisper, laugher's caught.
A splash here, a giggle there,
Mischief dances in the air.

With every heartbeat, the tension grows,
A twist of humor, everyone knows.
In the secret, the fun begins,
Beneath the surface, everyone grins.

A Symphony of Smirks

In the air, a tune of jest,
Crafted laughs, we know the best.
Strumming strings with joyful flair,
A symphony of smiles to share.

Each note a giggle, sharp and bright,
Dancing shadows come to light.
With every chuckle, the rhythm sways,
In perfect time, the humor plays.

Claps and snaps, the beat is sly,
As silly antics wave goodbye.
A chorus of giggles rises high,
While sparkles of humor float the sky.

Join the melody, don't delay,
In this concert of light-hearted play.
With every duet, laughter's flare,
A symphony crafted beyond compare.

Hidden Laughs in the Gloaming

In the gloaming, whispers creep,
Secrets of laughter, oh so deep.
Hiding behind corners, snickers bloom,
Filling the air with joy and zoom.

Every shadow holds a tale,
Of silly pranks and laughter's trail.
As giggles scatter, twilight paints,
A canvas with humor, pure and quaint.

Between the trees, a chuckle stirs,
Creating mischief, just like hers.
A glimmer here, a nudge and wink,
In the gloaming, they laugh and think.

So when the sun drops, don't go to sleep,
For in the dusk, the laughter leaps.
With every hush, a chuckle flies,
Hidden laughs are the evening's prize.

Masks of Mirth and Mischief

With smiles that twist, and laughter bright,
We come alive in the dim twilight.
Each jest a spark, each giggle a tease,
In this carnival of folly, we aim to please.

Oh, how we prance in our merry disguise,
With winks and nods, and playful lies.
A wink to the left, a grin to the right,
In our balmy banquet, we take flight.

Tickles and jabs, we're full of cheer,
With every tease, we draw near.
In this masquerade, where humor thrives,
We dance through the night, feeling so alive.

So join the fun, let the games begin,
With laughter as fuel, we'll surely win.
In masks of mirth, we'll spin and play,
Chasing the gloom, come what may.

The Art of Playful Provocation

A cheeky grin and a call to jest,
We stir the pot, putting humor to the test.
With words like arrows, we aim for hearts,
Crafting our mischief, where laughter starts.

In the game of banter, we lead with flair,
With clever quips that float in the air.
Like jesters in court, we jive and weave,
Provoking smiles, it's hard to believe.

With playful nudges and swift retorts,
We build a kingdom of fun in our forts.
Each poke a spark that ignites the night,
In this playful chaos, everything's right.

So gather 'round, let the laughter ring,
In this art of mischief, we take wing.
With every chuckle, we brighten the day,
In a world of jests, we will sway.

Daring Dances in Dim Light

With each sideways glance comes a daring chance,
Of mischief and mayhem in a nimble dance.
The lights may twinkle, but our eyes are bright,
As we tango through tales that gleefully bite.

In shadowy corners, we plot and scheme,
With laughter as our guide, we follow the dream.
With each twirl, a giggle, a sly little wink,
In the dimmest of hours, we dare not blink.

A shuffle, a jig, our spirits take flight,
Together we spin, with hearts so light.
Embracing the chaos, we let it unfold,
In these daring dances, our stories are told.

So let the stars witness our cheeky parade,
As we strut through the night, unafraid.
In the realm of jest, we'll shine so bright,
In daring dances, we embrace the light.

Sarcasm's Silhouettes

In the corner of wit, where banter takes flight,
Sarcasm dances in the cool moonlight.
With every jab, we sport a sly grin,
Crafting our shadows, where humor begins.

The echoes of laughter, a sweet serenade,
As we charm with illusions, and laughs masquerade.
With phrases like daggers, we poke and we prod,
In this theater of jest, we're all applause, not a nod.

We twirl our words, like whispers at play,
Teasing each other in the silliest way.
A chorus of chuckles that twine through the air,
In the silhouettes of sarcasm, we dare.

So tip your hat to the jesters we are,
In this witty ballet, we're each a star.
With each clever line, let the laughter rise,
In the embrace of whimsy, we take to the skies.

Twilight Dialogues of the Playful

In twilight's glow, we play our tricks,
With giggles sprouting, like youthful flicks.
A whisper here, a jest nearby,
As fireflies dance and lovers sigh.

The moon's our stage, we act so bold,
With laughter's warmth, like tales retold.
A clownish wink, a playful shove,
Under the stars, we find our love.

Each line we toss, a feather's flight,
With snickers soft and laughter bright.
In shadowed corners, secrets bloom,
As joy ignites the dusky gloom.

In every jest, the heart's a song,
With playful banter, we all belong.
So come and join this merry dance,
In twilight's glow, we'll take a chance.

The Elegance of Enticing Banter

With winks of folly, we take our seats,
In nightly glow, where laughter meets.
A subtle tease, a sly remark,
With snappy comebacks, we light the dark.

The air's alive with light, sweet cheek,
In playful jabs, our spirits peek.
A glance exchanged, a giggle shared,
In tangled words, our hearts are bared.

As words pirouette like dancers bold,
Each sentence spun, a tale retold.
The humor drips from every line,
In elegance, our paths entwine.

So let us revel in this charade,
With teasing tones, we serenade.
In every laugh, a bond so dear,
In banter's embrace, we shift gear.

Mischievous Glimmers

In the corner lurks a playful sprite,
With mischievous glimmers, shining bright.
A wink from here, a nudge from there,
In silly whispers, we dance with air.

Stolen glances punctuate our play,
With every chuckle, we seize the day.
In jest we find a bubbling thrill,
In fleeting moments, joy's never still.

A playful poke, a teasing phrase,
In laughter's grip, we're lost for days.
With gleeful spirits, we weave our fate,
In hidden corners, our laughter waits.

So gather round, let the games commence,
With each sly giggle, we break the fence.
In mischief's twinkle, we share our cheer,
A world of laughter, just waiting here.

The Humor That Lurks

Behind the curtain, humor waits,
With giggles trapped at fortune's gates.
A tiny jest, a sipping sip,
In whispered tones, we let it rip.

The chuckles tumble, double back,
In each sly glance, a playful crack.
A jape, a poke, a cheeky line,
In humor's grasp, we intertwine.

The night's our canvas, fun unleashed,
With every laugh, our fears decreased.
In silly antics, mischief thrives,
In laughter's light, our spirit drives.

So let us dance with joy unfurled,
In playful banter, we spin the world.
With humor's power, we boldly stoke,
In every jest, our hearts evoke.

Eclipsed by Eloquent Escapades

In the alley where laughter roams,
Jesters dance, proclaiming homes.
With tricks and tales that gleefully play,
Time skips on a merry ballet.

A tumble here, a slip on the ground,
With winks and giggles, joy is found.
Puns like balloons float in the air,
Chasing woes with a playful flair.

Misdirection paints a comical scene,
Where chaos reigns but feels so keen.
Beneath the neon's gleaming sight,
We find ourselves lost in delight.

With every jest, a snicker flows,
In the carnival of what life bestows.
So let's embrace this silly chase,
In the world of humorous grace.

The Sassy Veil of Dusk's Charm.

When twilight dresses in cheeky hues,
A parade of giggles walks in twos.
With every flicker, a smile ignites,
We dance through folly on starry nights.

Charmed whispers echo in the breeze,
As laughter swells beneath the trees.
A wink, a nod, the moon grins wide,
In this realm where fun can't hide.

Jokes on the wind, they dash and dart,
Daring us to join the art.
With every pun, a sparkle flies,
Turning our woes into clownish sighs.

So don your cap with playful pride,
In the escapade where quirks abide.
For dusk invites mischief, it seems,
Wrapping us snug in silly dreams.

Whispers of Witty Contrasts

In the gallery of life's grand design,
Laughs collide, bursting like wine.
With irony's brush, we paint the day,
Every flaw turned jest, in a comical play.

Sneaky grins cross mischievous lanes,
While puns dissolve our worldly pains.
In the realm of quirks, where antics thrive,
We jest and jive, oh how we strive.

A riddle jests, a pun gets bold,
Chortles echo, never growing old.
In witticisms where wisdom bends,
Laughter's the magic that never ends.

With vibrant jesters strutting wide,
Each quirk an adventure, on this ride.
It's in these whispers, silly and bright,
We find our gold in sheer delight.

Laughter's Veil

In the tapestry of whimsical tales,
Giggles weave through vibrant trails.
With a belly laugh that never tires,
Foolishness dances around like fires.

A grin here, a chuckle there,
The world transforms in this silly air.
Whimsy prances, skipping with glee,
As we tumble through jests, wild and free.

Silliness glows in the moonlit night,
While riddle and rhyme take flight.
With every grin, a spark ignites,
In the carnival of foolish delights.

So gather, my friends, let the fun unfold,
Where laughter's veil never grows old.
In the symphony of jokes, we thrive,
Together in joy, we come alive.

The Art of Sly Grins

A wink and a nod, how sly it can be,
Crafting a joke, as light as a breeze.
With laughter in eyes, we play the game,
Hidden in giggles, we flourish in fame.

A smirk on the face, it dances with flair,
Whispers of mischief float in the air.
Pulling a prank, with glee we ignite,
Those sly little grins, a true delight!

A flick of a brow, the jesters' parade,
In moments of joy, our worries do fade.
Tickles and jests wrapped snugly in rhyme,
The art of sly grins transcending all time.

With sparkly eyes and a feigned surprise,
The jest must be clever, oh what a prize!
In the heart of the jest, we find purest fun,
A canvas of laughter, forever undone.

Echoes of Playful Sarcasm

In echoes of laughter, we toss words in jest,
Playfully aiming to ruffle and test.
With a wink and a nudge, we let the fun flow,
Finding joy in the cracks, where we giggle and glow.

A twist of the tongue, how it dances and sways,
Each quip like a blossom on sun-soaked days.
The punchlines we weave, like vines intertwined,
Planting smiles so deep, they're almost enshrined.

With sarcasm rich, like a chocolate delight,
We feast on our words under soft, starry light.
A tickle of humor, an art form, it's true,
Echoing laughter, a world made anew.

From snarky remarks to playful debate,
Our hearts line the shelves with memories so great.
In the timbre of voices, a legacy drawn,
In echoes of humor, we dance until dawn.

Glistening Glares

When eyes emit sparks, like raindrops of cheer,
With glistening glares, they whisper, "Come near!"
A look full of mischief, a knowing glance shared,
In moments unguarded, hilarity bared.

What's brewing beneath that playful facade?
A canvas of jokes, blanketed by nods.
With a flicker of light, all senses collide,
In glistening glares, we unleash what we hide.

A twinkle, a sparkle, igniting the air,
The secret of laughter, our only declared.
In the depths of the night, we weave and we swerve,
With glistening glares, we gladly observe.

Adventures of jest in the gaze of a friend,
A radiant moment, unplanned and unbend.
In the glow of our humor, let worries be bare,
For life's just a ride, and we're strapped in with flair.

The Dance of Cheeky Reflections

In mirrors of humor, we glance and we stare,
Cheeky reflections, a playful affair.
With every coy smile that twirls in the light,
We dance with our quirks until day meets the night.

Jokes leap like shadows, we sway to the tune,
In cheeky reflections, we bubble like moon.
With winks that sparkle, the mischief we share,
The softness of laughter, light as the air.

A jig on the floor of our thoughts and delight,
With toes that tap swiftly, we keep spirits bright.
In the dance of our glee, we let every line,
Create the joyous rhythm of fate intertwined.

So come join the frolic, the jest, and the cheer,
In cheeky reflections, mischief draws near.
With giggles and grins, our hearts gently sway,
Celebrating the joy in the silliest way.

The Festival of Winks

The townsfolk gather, smiles so wide,
With playful jests, they twist and glide.
Each wink a secret, a playful tease,
As laughter echoes through the trees.

With juggling clowns and pies that fling,
Each face they meet knows how to sing.
A spark of joy, in every glance,
In this little carnival, we all dance.

The silly hats are tilted high,
While silly songs make spirits fly.
They swap the cheese for jelly beans,
And challenge fate with goofy scenes.

The festival turns from day to night,
As fireflies join in the delight.
In every corner, smiles ignite,
Where joy blooms wildly, taking flight.

Light-Hearted Fancies

In a world where whims come out to play,
The bunnies hop in a silly ballet.
A parade of ducks, in hats afashioned,
With every quack, our hearts are rationed.

Pies in the air, oh what a sight!
The frolicsome cake, its frosting so bright.
Unruly giggles hang in the air,
As ticklish squabbles become a dare.

Each wink and nudge, a plot unfolds,
In light-hearted tales that humor molds.
Between the laughter, joy will swell,
In every moment, a magic spell.

With merry tunes, they dance and twirl,
In a giggling, spinning, crazy whirl.
As the sun dips low, tonight's at play,
We'll chase the frowns delight away.

Hidden Grins in the Night

When moonbeams shimmer, soft and light,
Mischief stirs in the velvet night.
A snoozing cat with dreams to chase,
While shadows dance at a lively pace.

With whispered jokes and giggles shared,
Under the stars, the night is dared.
A sneaky sprite behind the trees,
Tickles the ribs with a playful breeze.

The specters play, in their ghostly glee,
In the echoes of laughter, wild and free.
Each rustle spruces, in laughter's grip,
As night unfolds its comic script.

With scurrying feet on the cobblestone,
Joyful secrets, we make our own.
In hidden corners, it's pure delight,
As we share grins in the deep, dark night.

Guile and Giggles

A clever fox with a waggish grin,
Crafting tricks with a playful spin.
Tales spin round, in whispers told,
Of tangled webs, and jokes so bold.

At every turn, a prank awaits,
With playful twists that test our fates.
A sneaky grin, a knowing glance,
Inviting all into this dance.

The baffled bear in a hat so grand,
Waddling forth, just as he planned.
Each chuckle shared, a treat of mirth,
In their madcap search for giggling worth.

In a world of whims, both sly and spry,
Where laughter reigns, and spirits fly.
With every guile that's aimed for fun,
The magic of giggles has just begun.

Flickers of Follies at Dusk

When twilight chuckles, the world grows bold,
Jokes unfurl like petals, secrets unfold.
Giggling whispers dance on the breeze,
Follies emerge, put minds at ease.

Laughter flickers where fun takes flight,
Pranks in the shadows weave through the night.
Twinkling stars join in with glee,
As silliness reigns, wild and free.

With a wink and a grin, the mischief starts,
Toying with giggles, amusing hearts.
In the dusk, where quirks come alive,
We twirl in joy, and laughter thrives.

The moon casts light on playful scenes,
In this realm of chuckles, nothing's as it seems.
So come join the fun, let laughter abide,
In flickering follies where cheer cannot hide.

Shadows that Sparkle with Sass

In corners where mischief is often found,
Sassy secrets in shadows abound.
With a jolt and a jiggle, they twirl about,
Crafting cheeky stories, banters sprout.

Watch out for the glares of playful eyes,
Witty remarks and quick, clever lies.
With every step, there's a burst of jest,
In these spirited realms, we're simply blessed.

The sparkle of sass makes everything bright,
As giggles erupt under the moonlight.
Oh, the tales that unfold in the dark,
Every playful jab is a shimmering spark.

Each shadow dances with vibrant flair,
In a world where silliness dominates the air.
So let your heart jump to the rhythms of fun,
In a realm of sass where laughter's begun.

Gleeful Glimmers of Quirk

Twists and turns in the evening glow,
Gleeful glimmers put on a show.
Witty banter flying high,
As humor flutters and passes by.

In the glow of quirks, surprises await,
With every giggle, we contemplate.
Silly tales spun in the moon's embrace,
A playground of quirks, a lively space.

With hopscotch dreams and butterfly cheer,
We dance in laughter, casting off fear.
Every glance tells a story of fun,
In this quirky realm, we all are one.

So leap into mirth, let your spirit sing,
Every corner's a treasure, a whimsical fling.
In gleeful glimmers, we find our place,
Where smiles thrive and joy we embrace.

Murmurs of the Cheeky Shade

In the cool of the night where laughter spills,
Murmurs of mischief churn through the hills.
In shadows that twinkle and tease with glee,
A place of delight, just you and me.

Whispers of fun play tricks on the ear,
Cheeky banter that draws us near.
Every jest is a spark of delight,
As we frolic in humor throughout the night.

Larks in the dusk, where silliness calls,
With a wink and a nod, we break down the walls.
In this playful hush, we giggle and slip,
With every soft chuckle, we take a trip.

So gather 'round, for the fun won't fade,
In the murmur of night, where memories are made.
Let's revel in laughter, as joy takes its aim,
In this cheeky shade, we're all one and the same.

The Artistry of Winks

In a room of giggles, a sly blink flies,
Each glance a secret, a glorious prize.
With a smirk from the corner, laughter ignites,
Witty retorts take off on their flights.

A nod, a grin, like a dance on a stage,
Everyone plays their part, nothing's a cage.
Jokes whispered low, like soft summer breeze,
Tickling the ears, bringing minds to their knees.

A flick of an eye, the crowd's in a spell,
They chime in together, in humor they dwell.
The art of the wink, a delightful embrace,
In this playful manner, we all find our place.

So raise up your glass to the jesters so true,
With laughter as paint, they create something new.
In the gallery of giggles, where fun is the king,
The artistry of winks makes our hearts take wing.

Moonlit Mockery

Under the glow of an evening so bright,
Funny tales wander, giving pure delight.
Peeking from corners, the wisecracks parade,
While laughter erupts, no moment is weighed.

Figures in shadows play tricks with the light,
Making us chuckle, oh what a sight!
With whispers and giggles, the night stretches wide,
Each jest that is tossed on a whimsical tide.

The moon, in its wisdom, rolls back its gaze,
As friends trade their banter in comical ways.
In this ballet of snickers, joy takes a leap,
Mockery dances while we're lost in our sleep.

So gather 'round folks, let the night be a tease,
For laughter's the treasure that puts hearts at ease.
In moonlit mockery, let worries unfurl,
And toast to the joys spun in this silly world.

The Pantomime of Jest

With grand gestures made in the flickering light,
Faces tell stories that sparkle and bite.
Each chuckle a flourish, each snicker a song,
In this pantomime dance, we all belong.

Eyes wide with wonder, the satire flows free,
Capsizing the mundane, with glee and esprit.
As hearts play the tune of a whimsical jest,
We weave through the laughter, feeling truly blessed.

A flip of the wrist, a twirl on the floor,
These antics invite smiles, and so much more.
Each mimed little struggle, each humorous plight,
Brings joy bubbling up, with comedic delight.

So let's raise our hands and applaud this fine art,
For the pantomime jesters, who play to our heart.
With laughter as canvas and friendship the thread,
We grasp every moment, and joy is widespread.

Laughter in the Shadows

In corners unnoticed, laughter sneaks by,
With whispers, tickles that flutter and fly.
Jokes wrapped in giggles, like secrets we keep,
In shadows they twinkle, where chuckles creep.

A tap on the shoulder, a wink in the night,
We dance in the dark, as the laughs take flight.
Every quip is a spark, lighting up the room,
Turning silence to symphonies, exuberance blooms.

The jesters unite with a clever façade,
Juggling stories that leave us all awed.
In this merry maze, sheer joy we discover,
While shadows conspire, we laugh and we buffer.

So gather your friends for a night full of cheer,
Where laughter in shadows is always sincere.
With punchlines and pranks, our hearts intertwine,
In this world of frolic, what magic we find!

Tricksters Treading Tender Lines

In a world of giggles and laughs,
They dance on the edge of the absurd,
With each step, a chuckle erupts,
Mischievous glee, how they've stirred.

Pranks hidden under a friendly guise,
A wink here, a nudge over there,
With every twist, the mind does spin,
Oh, the joy of their playful flair.

They tangle in jokes, a knot so tight,
But laughter sets the spirit free,
Each jibe and jest, a comic delight,
In this ballet of whimsy, we all agree.

So come along, let's share the jest,
In this frolic of fun, we shall bask,
For in the realm of tricksters' test,
The heart is light, and smiles unmask.

Nimbus of Naïveté and Nuance

In a haze of giggles, bliss prevails,
With a dash of sweet innocence mixed,
Like sugar on candy, and winks at trials,
Life's quirky puzzle is easily fixed.

Oh, the whimsy in each puzzled look,
What mischief dreams lurk in their eyes?
Their laughter's a tune from a children's book,
Dancing through life, where folly flies.

Every glance a riddle, every quip a clue,
They step lightly, joy in every stride,
With missteps that turn into laughter too,
In this playful realm, where grins abide.

Like sunbeams caught in a playful chase,
Laughter ignites the night's gentle grace,
Floating on humor, in a colorful space,
Naïveté and nuance, a merry embrace.

Laughter's Light in the Gloom

When the day's weighed down in a dreary frown,
A giggle slips through, soft as a sigh,
It bounces and dances, uplifting the town,
Like balloons on a breeze, soaring high.

With humor that glimmers like stars in the dark,
Each chuckle's a spark that ignites the night,
In shadows that linger, their shenanigans mark,
The canvas of gloom splashed with pure light.

So gather the jesters, the merry and bright,
With punchlines that twinkle and tickle the air,
In the heart of the gloom, find the jesting delight,
For laughter's the lantern that banishes care.

So let's paint our smiles with a splash of fun,
Turning frowns to mirth, till the day is done,
In laughter's warm glow, we're all surely won,
As joy takes the lead, and new tales are spun.

The Playful Echo of Nightfall

As dusk drapes the world in a velvet cloak,
A chorus of chuckles begins to unfurl,
Whispered giggles float, like innocent smoke,
In the twilight's embrace, mischief's a whirl.

With each rustle and hum, a tale is spun,
Of trick or treat, where puns come to play,
They leap from the darkness, like rays from the sun,
In this nighttime ballet, laughter holds sway.

The moon grins knowingly, a wink in its gleam,
While shadows are frolicking, crafty and bold,
In the playful echo of dreams, we all beam,
As stories unfold, a wonder retold.

So join in the quest, the jesters parade,
Where fun knows no bounds, and giggles renown,
In the blanket of night, we merrily wade,
In laughter's sweet echo, together we drown.

Twinkling Teasing

In the corner lurks a grin,
A pop of laughter tucked within.
Jesters dance on tiptoe feet,
While wisecracks bubble with a beat.

A wink shared with a sly delight,
Giggling softly in the night.
With silly hats and playful spins,
Everyone knows where the fun begins.

Whispers float with a cheeky flair,
As chuckles rise in the cool night air.
Every jest, a bright escape,
In the silence where giggles drape.

From the shadows come the roars,
Of laughs that fling open doors.
Each punchline crafted, light as air,
Crafts a world beyond compare.

The Glee in Gloom

When the clouds drape low and gray,
A snicker bubbles on the way.
Puns parade with raincoat flair,
Bringing joy to the dampened air.

With playful jabs and witty quips,
They dance around on joyful trips.
In every frown, a smile found,
Chasing gloom from its cold ground.

Umbrellas turned to shields of cheer,
Banter makes the storm disappear.
With every twirl and laugh so loud,
They find joy where shadows shroud.

Out of the gray, a melody sings,
While silliness on the raindrop swings.
Each glance a ticket to the show,
Where glee erupts, letting laughter grow.

Witty Silhouettes

Beneath the lamp's warm gentle glow,
Figures move in a playful flow.
Arms outstretched in jest and cheer,
Each shadow shares a happy sneer.

In corners sit the laughs amassed,
Recounting tales from the past.
Curved lines twist with every joke,
As laughter rises like a smoke.

Glimmers spark as the night unfolds,
Jam-packed with stories waiting to be told.
Every silhouette bursts with life,
In this joyful dance without strife.

Here friendships weave like threads of gold,
In the fun and laughter, brave and bold.
With every moment, a new delight,
As witty figures dance through the night.

The Glow of Humor in Dusk

As daylight fades to a soft embrace,
Smiles ignite each familiar face.
With every chuckle, spirits soar,
Filling the air with a hearty roar.

In the twilight's gentle hand,
Jokes take flight like grains of sand.
Echoes of laughter fill the trees,
Breezy banter carried by the breeze.

Lights twinkle with mischievous charm,
The night wraps all in a happy balm.
Wit ignites like stars in the sky,
As giggles float and never die.

The glow of humor paints the night,
Chasing away darkness with vibrant light.
In every jest, a shimmer of joy,
Creating warmth none could destroy.

www.ingramcontent.com/pod-product-compliance
Lightning Source LLC
Chambersburg PA
CBHW051632160426
43209CB00004B/619